A breakfast recipes cookbook is a comprehensive collection of delicious and easy-to-follow recipes that cater to breakfast lovers of all kinds. It features a variety of recipes for classic breakfast dishes, as well as innovative and unique dishes that are sure to tantalize your taste buds.

The cookbook typically starts with a brief introduction to breakfast and its importance in starting the day right. It may also provide an overview of essential ingredients and kitchen tools needed to make the recipes in the book. The recipes are organized into chapters, with each chapter focusing on a different type of breakfast dish such as eggs, pancakes, waffles, oatmeal, smoothies, and more.

Each recipe is accompanied by a beautiful photograph, a list of ingredients, and clear step-by-step instructions to guide you through the cooking process. Some cookbooks may also include tips and tricks for making the perfect breakfast, variations on classic recipes, and suggestions for ingredient substitutions to accommodate dietary restrictions.

Whether you're a busy professional looking for quick and easy breakfast ideas, a parent in search of healthy and kid-friendly options, or a food enthusiast eager to try new and exciting dishes, a breakfast recipes cookbook has something for everyone. From simple scrambled eggs to gourmet avocado toast, these recipes are designed to help you start your day on a delicious note.

Strawberry Toast

Strawberry Toast is a healthy and tasty breakfast option for kids that's easy to prepare. To make it, start by melting the butter in a medium-sized skillet over medium heat. Add the sliced strawberries and cook for 5 minutes or until the berries have softened. Next, add the maple syrup, orange zest, non-fat milk, and teaspoon of salt. Cook for another 3 minutes or until the mixture thickens. Finally, place the slices of cinnamon raisin bread in a single layer on top of the strawberry mixture. Crack three eggs over the toast and let cook until the whites are set and yolks have just started to become soft. Serve immediately with a sprinkle of extra orange zest. Enjoy!

Blueberry Muffins

Ingredients

1 ½ cups all-purpose flour. Great Value All-Purpose Flour, 5LB Bag.
¾ cup white sugar.
2 teaspoons baking powder.
½ teaspoon salt.
⅓ cup vegetable oil.
1 egg.
⅓ cup milk, or more as needed.
1 cup fresh blueberries.

Making a batch of delicious and healthy blueberry muffins is easy with the right ingredients. To begin, preheat your oven to 375°F (190°C). In a large bowl, combine 1 ½ cups all-purpose flour, ¾ cup white sugar, 2 teaspoons baking powder and ½ teaspoon salt. Add ⅓ cup vegetable oil and mix with a wooden spoon until the dry ingredients are moistened. Beat in 1 egg, then stir in ⅓ cup of milk. Gently fold in 1 cup fresh blueberries for a hint of sweetness and color.

Line your muffin tin with paper liners or spray it with cooking spray and fill each cup three-quarters full with the batter. Bake in preheated oven for 18 to 20 minutes, or until a toothpick inserted into the center of a muffin comes out clean. Let cool and enjoy your homemade blueberry muffins!

These healthy blueberry muffins are perfect as a snack or dessert, especially when baking with kids. They also make a great addition to a lunchbox and are sure to be a hit with the little ones! With this simple recipe, you can create tasty and nutritious treats in no time. So next time your family is looking for something sweet, whip up a batch of these blueberry muffins for an easy and healthy dessert.
Enjoy!

Coconut Yogurt Cake

Ingredients:

2 eggs
¾ cup (180ml) light-flavoured extra virgin olive oil
1 cup (280g) natural Greek-style (thick) yoghurt
2 tablespoons lemon juice
½ cup (110g) caster (superfine) sugar
½ cup (180g) honey
1 cup (80g) desiccated coconut
1¼ cups (225g) white spelt flour
1 teaspoon baking powder
½ teaspoon baking soda
½ teaspoon salt

Instructions:

Preheat the oven to 160°C/320°F.

Grease and line a 22cm round cake tin.

In a large mixing bowl, beat the eggs until light and fluffy.

Add the olive oil, yoghurt, lemon juice, caster sugar, and honey to the bowl, and whisk until well combined.

Fold in the desiccated coconut.

In a separate bowl, sift the spelt flour, baking powder, baking soda, and salt.

Gradually fold the flour mixture into the egg mixture until just combined.

Pour the mixture into the prepared cake tin and smooth the surface with a spatula.

Bake in the preheated oven for 50-60 minutes, or until a skewer inserted into the center of the cake comes out clean.

Remove the cake from the oven and allow it to cool in the tin for 10 minutes.

Turn the cake out onto a wire rack and allow it to cool completely.

Serve the coconut yoghurt cake with a dollop of Greek yoghurt and fresh berries on top.

Enjoy your delicious Coconut Yoghurt Cake!

Chocolate Avocado Mousse

Avocado and chocolate mousse is a delicious no sugar dessert recipe that is also healthy. To make this decadent treat, you will need two ripe avocados chopped, 200g of good quality dark eating chocolate (60-75% cocoa) broken into pieces, ½ cup of your preferred milk of choice such as cow's, almond or coconut milk, and two tablespoons of liquid honey or pure maple syrup (optional).

To prepare the mousse, first melt the chocolate in a heatproof bowl over simmering water or in a microwave. Once melted, set aside to cool slightly. In a food processor combine the avocados and stir with melted chocolate until combined and smooth. Add milk and sweetener of choice to the mixture and blend together until light and creamy.

Transfer the mousse into separate bowls or glasses, cover with cling film, and refrigerate for 1-2 hours. When ready to eat, enjoy - this delicious no sugar dessert recipe is guilt-free! Enjoy!

You can also serve the mousse with some fresh berries or grated dark chocolate for a touch of sweetness. No matter how you choose to enjoy your avocado and chocolate mousse, it definitely is a healthy dessert that will satisfy all taste buds! Enjoy!

Banana Chia Pudding

INGREDIENTS

2 LARGE OVERRIPE BANANAS.
2 CUPS UNSWEETENED COCONUT (BEVERAGE), ALMOND OR CASHEW MILK.
6 TABLESPOONS CHIA SEEDS.

Banana Chia Pudding is a no sugar dessert recipe that anyone can prepare in no time at all! It's healthy and delicious, making it the perfect treat for any occasion. To make this tasty no-sugar dessert, you'll need two overripe bananas, two cups of unsweetened coconut (beverage), almond or cashew milk, and six tablespoons of chia seeds. First, mash the bananas in a bowl until no lumps remain. Add the milk and stir to combine. Then add the chia seeds and stir again until everything is mixed together well. Cover the bowl with plastic wrap and place it in the refrigerator for a few hours or overnight. Once the chia pudding has thickened and all of the ingredients have blended together, you can enjoy it! Serve it with fresh fruit or your favorite topping. Banana Chia Pudding is a no sugar dessert recipe that's sure to satisfy any sweet tooth! Enjoy!

Egg Muffins

When it comes to baking, there are many options to choose from that will tantalize your taste buds. From cakes and cupcakes, to muffins and brownies, there's something for everyone. But one of the most popular treats is the classic egg muffin. Egg muffins are quick and easy to make and perfect for breakfast on-the-go. Here's what you'll need:

- -Eggs
- -Milk
- -Cheese
- -Veggies of your choice (onion, bell peppers, mushrooms, spinach are all great options)
- -Butter or oil for cooking
- -Salt and pepper to taste.

Start by preheating the oven to 375 degrees F and greasing a muffin pan with butter or oil. In a large bowl, whisk together eggs, milk, cheese and veggies. Fill each muffin cup about 3/4 full with egg mixture and season with salt and pepper to taste. Bake for 25 minutes or until egg is set. Enjoy! With egg muffins you can have a delicious breakfast ready in no time

Scrambled Eggs

Eggs are one of the best sources of protein to start the day and scrambled eggs take just minutes to make. Just whisk eggs with milk, season with salt and pepper, and fry them in a non-stick pan for an easy breakfast that your child will love.

Baked Donuts

Are you looking for a delicious and healthy dessert that kids are sure to love? Baked donuts might be the perfect treat! To make them, you'll need some simple ingredients: 4 tablespoons (57g) of butter, 1/4 cup (50g) of vegetable oil, 1/2 cup (99g) of granulated sugar, 1/3 cup (71g) of light brown sugar or dark brown sugar packed, 2 large eggs, 1 1/2 teaspoons baking powder, 1/4 teaspoon baking soda and ½ to 1 teaspoon nutmeg.

To prepare the donuts, preheat your oven to 350°F (175°C). In a medium-sized bowl, cream together the butter and sugars until light and fluffy. Add in the eggs one at a time, beating well after each addition. In a separate bowl, mix together all of the dry ingredients - baking powder, baking soda and nutmeg. Gradually add the dry ingredients to the wet ingredients, mixing until combined.

Using a spoon, drop the dough into lightly greased donut pans. Bake for 8 to 10 minutes, or until golden brown. Let the donuts cool completely before serving. Enjoy! Baked donuts are a fun and tasty treat that kids will love, and they're great for healthy dessert recipes too!

Rice Chocolate Pudding

Ingredients
1/3 cup medium-grain rice.
1/4 cup cocoa powder.
3 1/4 cups skim milk.
1/4 cup caster sugar.
canned pears, to serve.

Here's the method to go along with the ingredients:

Rinse the rice and place it in a medium-sized saucepan with 1 1/2 cups of water. Bring to a boil, then reduce the heat to low and simmer for 15 minutes, or until the rice is cooked and the water has been absorbed.
Add the cocoa powder, milk and sugar to the saucepan and stir to combine. Place the pan over medium heat and cook for 10-15 minutes, stirring frequently, until the pudding thickens and the rice is very tender.
Divide the pudding between four serving dishes and chill in the fridge for at least 1 hour, or until set.
Serve the pudding with canned pears on top. Enjoy!

Oatmeal Pancakes

Ingredients:
- 1 cup old-fashioned rolled oats
- 1 cup milk, regular or non-dairy
- 2 large eggs
- 1 tablespoon unsalted butter, plus more for cooking
- 1 tablespoon granulated sugar
- 2/3 cup all-purpose flour
- 2 teaspoons baking powder
- 1/4 teaspoon kosher salt
- 1/4 teaspoon ground cinnamon (optional)

- **Instructions:**
- 1. In a medium bowl, combine the oats and milk and let stand for 10 minutes.
- 2. In a small bowl, whisk together the eggs, butter, and sugar until light and fluffy.
- 3. Add the egg mixture to the oats mixture and stir until combined.
- 4. In a separate bowl, sift together the flour, baking powder, salt, and cinnamon (if using).
- 5. Add the dry ingredients to the wet ingredients in two batches and mix until just combined - do not overmix!
- 6. Heat a non-stick frying pan over

Apple Nut Muffins

Ingredients:

2 cups all-purpose flour.
1/2 cup granulated sugar.
3 teaspoons baking powder.
1 1/2 teaspoon ground cinnamon, divided.
1/2 teaspoon salt.
2 eggs.
3/4 cup milk.
1 apple, peeled, cored, and finely chopped (about 1 cup)

These healthy snack muffins are a great way to get kids to enjoy healthy food. Not only are they easy to make, but they also have the added bonus of containing nutritious ingredients like apples, eggs and all-purpose flour.

To prepare these healthy snack muffins, start by preheating your oven to 375 degrees F. In a large bowl, whisk together the flour, sugar, baking powder, 1 teaspoon cinnamon and salt. In another bowl, beat together the eggs and milk until smooth. Then stir in the apple.

Next add the wet ingredients into the dry ingredients and mix until blended. Spoon the batter into greased or paper lined muffin cups filling them about two-thirds full. Sprinkle the remaining cinnamon over the top.

Bake for 18-20 minutes, or until a toothpick inserted into the center of the muffin comes out clean. Let cool before serving and enjoy! With these healthy snack muffins, your kids will love healthy food without even knowing it.

Happy snacking!

Breakfast Grilled Cheese

Grilled cheese sandwiches are a classic favorite, made of two slices of bread with melted cheese in the middle. But what if you want to take your grilled cheese up a notch? Try adding egg and sausage! Start by cooking some diced sausage in a pan until it's fully cooked through. Then, crack an egg into the same pan and scramble it with the sausage until both ingredients are thoroughly mixed together. Spread this egg-sausage mix onto half of one slice of bread and then cover it with plenty of grated cheese before adding another piece of bread on top. Place the sandwich in a heated skillet over medium heat for about 3 minutes each side or until the bread is golden brown and the cheese has melted completely. Enjoy this egg and sausage-filled grilled cheese sandwich with your favorite condiments

A grilled cheese sandwich is a simple and tasty meal. With egg and sausage added, it can be an even more delicious treat that the whole family will love. Don't forget to enjoy your egg and sausage grilled cheese sandwich!

Guacamole Toast

Ingredients:

- ripe avocados.
- Juice of 1 lime.
- 1/2 tsp. kosher salt.
- 1/2 c. cherry tomatoes, quartered.
- 1/2. small red onion, minced.
- 1/2. jalapeño, minced.
- clove garlic, minced.
- slices sourdough bread, toasted.

To make the guacamole, start by mashing the ripe avocados in a bowl. Add the juice of one lime and 1/2 teaspoon of kosher salt. Gently mix in the cherry tomatoes, red onion, jalapeño, and garlic. Serve your freshly made guacamole with slices of toasted sourdough bread for a delicious snack! Enjoy!

For an extra flavor boost, try adding diced mango or cilantro! The possibilities are endless! Whatever combination you choose will be sure to add some pizzazz to your homemade guacamole. Experiment away and share your creations with friends and family!

Happy snacking!

Apple Crisp

Ingredients

10 cups all-purpose apples, peeled, cored and sliced.
1 cup white sugar. Great Value Pure Granulated Sugar, 4 lb.
1 tablespoon all-purpose flour.
1 teaspoon ground cinnamon.
½ cup water.
1 cup quick-cooking oats.
1 cup all-purpose flour.
1 cup packed brown sugar.

Apple crisp is a delicious, healthy dish that makes for a great dessert recipe for kids. To prepare an apple crisp, you will need 10 cups of peeled and cored apples sliced into thin pieces. You can then combine the apples with 1 cup of white sugar, 1 tablespoon of all-purpose flour, 1 teaspoon of ground cinnamon, and ½ cup of water in a large bowl. In a separate bowl, combine 1 cup of quick-cooking oats, 1 cup of all-purpose flour and 1 cup of packed brown sugar. Sprinkle this mixture over the apples and mix it together gently until everything is evenly coated. Place the mixture into an 8x8 inch baking pan or dish and bake at 375 degrees Fahrenheit for 30-40 minutes until the top is golden brown. Enjoy your delicious apple crisp!

Apple crisp is a healthy dish that kids will love and it's easy to make. Not only does this recipe provide a great way for kids to get their daily intake of fruit, but it also provides them with the necessary vitamins and minerals they need to stay healthy. With just a few simple ingredients, you can make a delicious apple crisp that everyone will enjoy. So why not try out this tasty dessert recipe today? You won't regret it! Enjoy!

Apple Tart

225g/8oz Odlums Cream Plain Flour.
125g/4oz Butter or Margarine.
¼pt/150ml Cold Water (approx)
4 large Cooking Apples, peeled, cored and sliced.
Sugar, to sweeten apples.
Icing Sugar, to dust (optional)

Instructions for Apple Tart:

Preheat the oven to 190°C/375°F/Gas 5.
Rub the butter into the flour until it resembles breadcrumbs.
Add just enough cold water to bring the pastry together, but not too wet.
Roll out the pastry on a floured surface until it is large enough to cover a 20cm/8" round tart tin.
Line the tin with the pastry, trimming the edges and using a fork to prick the base.
Slice the apples and sweeten with sugar to taste. Arrange the apple slices on top of the pastry base.
Bake the apple tart in the preheated oven for about 30-35 minutes, until the pastry is golden brown and the apples are soft.
Allow the tart to cool before removing it from the tin.
Dust with icing sugar, if desired, before serving.

Pesto Quesadillas

If you're looking for vegetarian recipes for kids that are both healthy and delicious, try making these pesto quesadillas! Perfectly cheesy and packed with flavour, they'll become a family favourite in no time.

To make the pesto quesadillas, start by thinly slicing one roma tomato and gathering 3/4 cup of fresh baby spinach. Add 1/4 cup of vegan pesto to the vegetables; if desired, adjust this amount to suit your taste preferences. Next, add 1/2 cup of vegan mozzarella shreds (we recommend Follow Your Heart or Miyokos) as well as 1/4 cup of optional vegan feta crumbles. Place all of the ingredients onto two large tortillas (gluten-free if desired).

Once all of the ingredients are in place, carefully fold the tortillas over and press down to secure the ingredients. Preheat a skillet over medium heat and lightly grease with oil or vegan butter. Place the quesadilla onto the hot skillet and cook for 1-2 minutes on each side until golden brown. Finally, slice into wedges and serve warm!

Your vegetarian kids will love these delicious pesto quesadillas! Enjoy as a main dish, healthy lunchbox treat, or snack. Bon appetite!

Pumpkin Pie

INGREDIENTS

1 (15-OUNCE) CAN PUMPKIN PUREE.
1 (12-OUNCE) CAN EVAPORATED MILK.
3 LARGE EGGS.
3/4 CUP GRANULATED ARTIFICIAL SWEETENER, SUCH AS SPLENDA OR TRUVIA.
1 TEASPOON GROUND CINNAMON.
1/2 TEASPOON GROUND GINGER.
1/4 TEASPOON GROUND NUTMEG.
1/4 TEASPOON SALT.

Pumpkin pie is a classic no sugar dessert recipe that can be enjoyed any time of the year. It's a healthy alternative to other high-sugar desserts, and it won't break the calorie bank. Preparing a pumpkin pie is easy with just a few simple steps.

First, preheat your oven to 350°F and grease a 9-inch pie pan.

In a large bowl, mix together 1 (15-ounce) can of pumpkin puree, 1 (12-ounce) can evaporated milk, 3 large eggs, 3/4 cup granulated artificial sweetener such as Splenda or Truvia, 1 teaspoon ground cinnamon, 1/2 teaspoon ground ginger, 1/4 teaspoon ground nutmeg, and 1/4 teaspoon salt. Whisk everything together until combined.

Pour the mixture into the prepared pie pan and bake for 50-55 minutes or until a knife inserted into the center of the pie comes out clean. Let cool before serving. Enjoy!

Peanut Butter Pancakes

Ingredients

250g crunchy peanut butter.
50g unsalted butter, cubed, plus extra for cooking.
6 tbsp maple syrup.
300g self-raising flour.
1 tsp baking powder.
1 tbsp golden caster sugar.
2 large eggs.
350ml milk.

1. In a medium saucepan, melt the peanut butter and butter over low-medium heat until completely combined.
2. Add in the maple syrup, stirring frequently until fully incorporated. Set aside to cool slightly.
3. Combine the flour, baking powder and sugar in a large bowl and stir to combine.
4. In a separate bowl whisk together the eggs and milk until light and frothy, then add this to the dry ingredients along with the cooled peanut butter mixture. Stir together until just combined; don't over mix as this will make your pancakes tough!
5. Heat a non-stick frying pan over medium heat and lightly grease

Yogurt Muffins

Ingredients

2 cups (275g) good quality flour.
2 tsp. baking powder.
1/2 tsp baking soda.
pinch of salt.
1/2 cup (100g) sugar.
2 eggs.
1/2 cup (100ml) light olive oil.
1 cup (250ml) unsweetened yogurt (if using Greek yogurt, add 1 tbsp milk or buttermilk)

We all know how difficult it is to find healthy dessert recipes for kids. But, that doesn't mean you can't make delicious treats that are both tasty and nutritious! These Yogurt Muffins are sure to be a hit with the entire family.

To prepare these muffins, start by preheating your oven to 350°F (180°C). In a large bowl, combine the flour, baking powder, baking soda, and salt. In a separate bowl, mix together the sugar, eggs and oil. Add this mixture to the dry ingredients in the other bowl and stir until just combined.

Now add the yogurt and fold into the batter until it's just combined. Lightly grease a muffin tin and fill each cup with the batter. Bake for 18-20 minutes, or until a toothpick inserted into the center comes out clean. Let cool before serving.

These Yogurt Muffins are a great healthy dessert option that your kids will love! Enjoy!

Waffles

Ingredients

1 ¾ cups unbleached all purpose flour.
1 tablespoon baking powder.
1 tablespoon sugar.
½ teaspoon salt.
3 eggs.
8 tablespoon butter melted and cooled to room temp. I like to use the olive oil and butter blend sticks.
1 ½ cups 2% milk.

Waffles are a great and healthy breakfast for kids! Start by gathering all the ingredients you need: 1 ¾ cups unbleached all purpose flour, 1 tablespoon baking powder, 1 tablespoon sugar, ½ teaspoon salt, 3 eggs, 8 tablespoons butter melted and cooled to room temperature (you can use an olive oil and butter blend sticks), and 1 ½ cups 2% milk. In a medium bowl mix together the flour, baking powder, sugar and salt. In a separate bowl whisk together the eggs and then add in the melted butter and milk. Pour this egg mixture over the dry ingredients while whisking until completely blended. Now your waffle batter is ready to be cooked! Heat up your waffle maker according to its instructions and pour some of the batter in. After a few minutes you'll have delicious and healthy waffles for your kids to enjoy! Enjoy!

Enjoying waffles is a great way to start the day off on the right foot with a healthy breakfast for your kids. With just a few ingredients, you can whip up a batch of delicious waffles that will be sure to please even the pickiest of eaters. By following our simple instructions you'll be able to create tasty and nutritious waffles in no time! So what are you waiting for? Get cooking and enjoy this yummy breakfast treat!

Quesadillas

Ingredients
- 1 whole-grain flour tortilla (about 8″ diameter)
- ½ cup freshly grated cheddar cheese.
- ¼ cup cooked black beans or pinto beans, rinsed and drained.
- 1 tablespoon chopped red bell pepper or jarred roasted bell pepper or a few thinly sliced cherry tomatoes.
- 1 tablespoon chopped red onion or green onion.

Quesadillas are a healthy and delicious breakfast option for kids. With only four ingredients, it is easy to prepare with minimal effort. To make quesadillas, begin by taking one whole-grain flour tortilla (about 8″ diameter) and spreading ½ cup freshly grated cheddar cheese over one side of the tortilla. Then add ¼ cup cooked black beans or pinto beans, rinsed and drained, 1 tablespoon chopped red bell pepper or jarred roasted bell pepper, and 1 tablespoon chopped red onion or green onion on top of the cheese. Lastly, fold the un-cheese side of the tortilla onto the cheese side. Heat a skillet over medium heat and cook until both sides are golden brown and the cheese is melted. Cut into wedges and enjoy! Quesadillas are a healthy, protein-packed breakfast that kids will love!

Alternatively, you can also prepare quesadilla fillings ahead of time and store in the fridge for quickly assembling in the morning. Fill your tortilla with ¼ cup cooked black beans or pinto beans, rinsed and drained, 1 tablespoon chopped red bell pepper or jarred roasted bell pepper, 1 tablespoon chopped red onion or green onion and ½ cup freshly grated cheddar cheese. Wrap each filled tortilla in plastic wrap and place in an airtight container. In the morning, just heat up one quesadilla per person at a time until golden brown and serve

Classic Eggs Benedict

Ingredients

1 1/2 tablespoons white vinegar
8 large eggs
8 ounces thinly sliced smoked ham
4 English muffins (split and toasted)
2 tablespoons chopped fresh chives

Egg Benedict is a classic dish that is sure to please the whole family. The combination of healthy ingredients, such as smoked ham, eggs and English muffins, create a delicious and nutritious breakfast. Kids will love the flavor of this simple meal and it provides them with important sources of protein and vitamins. Plus, you can easily customize Egg Benedict by adding fresh herbs such as chives or substituting the smoked ham for bacon or turkey. Just don't forget the white vinegar which helps give this dish its signature flavor! With just a few ingredients, you can quickly whip up an amazing egg benedict breakfast that your kids will love!

Instructions

1. In a medium bowl, whisk together 1 1/2 tablespoons white vinegar and 8 large eggs.
2. Heat a wide non-stick pan over medium heat and add the egg mixture when it is hot. Cook for 2 minutes until the bottom layer has set before stirring gently with a spatula to scramble the eggs. Cook until all of the eggs are cooked through and set aside in a warm place
3. Toast 4 English muffins in a toaster or under the broiler until golden brown and cut each into halves. Place each half onto individual plates.
4. Place 8 ounces thinly sliced smoked ham on top of the toasted English muffins.
5. Divide the cooked eggs among the four plates and sprinkle with 2 tablespoons chopped fresh chives.
6. Serve warm and enjoy!

Fried Eggs And Bacon

Ingredients

4 large eggs.
8 bacon slices.
Kosher salt and freshly ground black pepper.
Toast, for serving.

Are you looking for an easy, healthy breakfast for your kids? Look no further than this delicious bacon and fried egg dish! It's packed with healthy protein and fats to give them the boost they need in the morning. Plus, it takes just minutes to prepare.

To make this healthy breakfast, start by frying 8 bacon slices over medium-high heat until crisp. Transfer the cooked bacon slices to a plate lined with paper towels to absorb any excess fat. Then, crack 4 large eggs into the hot pan and season with kosher salt and freshly ground black pepper. Fry on both sides until lightly browned and done to your liking. Serve immediately with toast for an easy yet healthy breakfast that will keep them full throughout the morning. Enjoy!

Scrambled Eggs Wrap!

Ingredients

1 or 2 large eggs.
1 or 2 tbsp milk (2%) or water.
Salt.
Pepper.
1-2 tbsp canola oil.
1 flour tortilla (8 inch)
2 tbsp shredded Cheddar cheese.
1 tbsp salsa.

Scrambled eggs wraps make a healthy and easy breakfast for kids. To prepare the wrap, start by cracking the eggs into a bowl. Add the milk (or water) and season with salt and pepper to taste. Heat oil in a non-stick pan over medium heat. Pour in the egg mixture and stir until scrambled, then remove from heat. Place tortilla on a flat surface and sprinkle with cheese, then spoon salsa onto one half of it. Add scrambled eggs to the other side of tortilla, fold it over and press lightly to seal. Enjoy! This tasty wrap can be served hot or cold, so it's perfect for busy mornings when you need something nutritious quickly!

Quiche with Spinach And Cheese

Ingredients

1/2 recipe homemade pie crust*
1 (10 oz) box frozen spinach*
8 oz fresh mushrooms, sliced.
1 teaspoon minced garlic (or roasted & chopped)
4 large eggs.
1 cup whole milk*
1/3 cup grated parmesan cheese.
1 cup shredded cheese (I used cheddar + mozzarella)*

Quiche with spinach and cheese is a healthy breakfast option that's simple to prepare. With only a few ingredients, you can have this tasty dish ready in no time! The combination of greens and cheese make it an ideal dish for kids. To get started, preheat your oven to 375°F (190°C).

Begin by preparing the pie crust according to recipe instructions or using store-bought pastry. Once the crust is ready, spread the frozen spinach evenly over the bottom of the tart shell. Then top with mushrooms and garlic.

In a medium bowl, whisk together eggs, milk and parmesan cheese until combined. Pour egg mixture over vegetables in crust then sprinkle shredded cheese on top. Place quiche on a baking sheet and bake for 25 minutes or until the center is set and cheese is golden brown.

Allow quiche to cool slightly before serving. Enjoy!

Almond Banana Muffins

INGREDIENTS

BANANA MUFFINS ULTRA-FINE ALMOND FLOUR –
SALT
BAKING POWDER OR USE 1 TEASPOON OF BAKING SODA
INSTEAD.
CINNAMON
MASHED BANANAS – THE BEST ARE RIPE BANANAS TO
ADD LOTS OF BANANA FLAVOR AND AVOID ADDING ANY
SWEETENER IN THE RECIPE.
LARGE EGGS AT ROOM TEMPERATURE
COCONUT OIL OR MELTED BUTTER
VANILLA EXTRACT
STEVIA DROPS OR 1/3 CUP OF GRANULATED SWEETENER
OF CHOICE

These muffins are so good, you won't even miss the sugar! ripe bananas add natural sweetness and moisture, while almond flour and coconut oil keep them tender and rich.

To make them, simply combine all of the ingredients in a bowl and mix until well combined. Then, spoon the batter into a muffin tin and bake at 350 degrees F for about 20 minutes.

These almond banana muffins are a delicious and healthy dessert option - perfect for those looking for no sugar dessert recipes! If you want to add more sweetness, you can always drizzle with honey or maple syrup. Enjoy!

English Breakfast

A healthy breakfast for kids doesn't have to be complicated or time consuming. A classic English breakfast can be a great option, providing all of the necessary nutrients for growing children in an enjoyable way. All you need is bacon, eggs, sausage, black pudding (optional), baked beans, grilled tomatoes and fried bread or toast. Serve it with healthy accompaniments such as jams, marmalades and fresh orange juice. When preparing an English breakfast for kids ensure that the ingredients are cooked properly and that any meat products are well done before serving. Breakfast is a key meal of the day so take your time to make sure you provide healthy options for your family. The traditional English breakfast can be a nutritious start to their day!

Tofu Scramble

Ingredients

1 tablespoon olive oil.
(1) 16-ounce block firm tofu.
2 tablespoons nutritional yeast.
1/2 teaspoon salt, or more to taste.
1/4 teaspoon turmeric.
1/4 teaspoon garlic powder.
2 tablespoons non-dairy milk, unsweetened and unflavored.

ofu scramble is a healthy breakfast for kids that can be easily prepared with just a few ingredients. To make the tofu scramble, first heat the olive oil in a non-stick skillet over medium-high heat. Next, crumble the block of firm tofu into small pieces and add it to the pan. Stir in the nutritional yeast, salt, turmeric, garlic powder and non-dairy milk. Cook for about 8 minutes or until desired texture is reached. Serve with cooked vegetables such as bell peppers, onions and mushrooms for extra flavor and nutrition. Enjoy!

Tofu scramble is an easy way to start your day off healthy while providing your children with all the essential nutrients they need to keep their energy levels up

Smoked Salmon Toast

Ingredients
1 ripe avocado.
1 tablespoon crème fraîche.
1 lemon.
70 g radishes.
3 sprigs of fresh dill.
1 tablespoon cider vinegar.
12-16 slices of crispbread or thinly sliced and toasted rye bread.
200 g smoked salmon, from sustainable sources.

Smoked Salmon Toast is a healthy and delicious breakfast option for kids. It's easy to prepare, with just a few simple ingredients - ripe avocado, crème fraîche, lemon, radishes, fresh dill, cider vinegar, crispbread or thinly sliced and toasted rye bread and smoked salmon.

To make the toast: Start by slicing the avocado into thin slices and arranging them on top of the toast. Mix together the crème fraîche with some freshly squeezed lemon juice until combined. Spread this mixture over the avocado slices. Slice the radishes into thin rounds and arrange them around each slice of toast. Sprinkle some finely chopped dill onto each slice of toast. Drizzle over some cider vinegar and top with some smoked salmon.

Serve the Smoked Salmon Toast for a healthy and delicious breakfast for kids. Enjoy!

Cottage Cheese Pancakes

INGREDIENTS

1 1/2 CUPS COTTAGE CHEESE
4 EGGS
1 TSP VANILLA EXTRACT
2 TBSP SUGAR
1 TBSP BAKING POWDER
1 CUP FLOUR
1/4 CUP CANOLA OIL

To begin making your cottage cheese pancakes, whisk together the cottage cheese and eggs until all the lumps are gone. Then add in the vanilla extract, sugar, baking powder and flour. Whisk until everything is well incorporated. Finally add in the canola oil and mix until combined.

Heat a skillet to medium heat and pour 1/4 cup of the batter onto the pan. Cook until small bubbles start to form around the edge, then carefully flip over with a spatula and cook for another 2-3 minutes. Serve your cottage cheese pancakes hot with butter or syrup. Enjoy!

These healthy pancakes are sure to provide your kids with the energy they need for their busy days ahead. You can even add in some fruit, nuts or chocolate chips for an extra special treat! With just a few simple steps you can have a healthy breakfast ready in no time. Give them a try today!

I want to take a moment to express my heartfelt gratitude for your recent purchase of my recipe book. As a passionate food lover, nothing makes me happier than sharing my favorite recipes with others. Your decision to invest in my book not only supports my dream, but also shows your commitment to expanding your culinary horizons.

I sincerely hope that the recipes in the book will inspire you to try new things and add some excitement to your meals.

Thank you again for your support and for being a part of this journey with me. I hope my book will bring you many happy and delicious moments in the kitchen.

www.ingramcontent.com/pod-product-compliance
Lightning Source LLC
Chambersburg PA
CBHW041151110526
44590CB00027B/4190